How to Make Money Online from home - Constant Continuity Cash

by Dan J. Brown

Affiliate Marketing For Beginners
The Simple Super-Affiliate Fieldbook
By Dan Brown

Published by:

Kirkland Publishing
11 Cavalier, Suite A-11
Montreal, QC, H9J1M6
514-608-6737 - phone
danbrown@danbrown.tv
www.danbrown.tv

All Rights Reserved. No part of this publication may be reproduced in any form or by any means, including scanning, photocopying, or otherwise without prior written permission of the copyright holder.

Copyright © 2014

Publisher's Note:
This publication is designed to provide accurate and authoritative information in regard to the subject matter covered. It is sold with the understanding that the publisher is not engaged in rendering legal, accounting or other professional services. If you require legal advice or other expert guidance, you should seek the services of a competent professional.

Without limiting the rights under copyright reserved above no part of this publication may be reproduced, stored in or introduced into a retrieval system, or transmitted, in any form or by any means (electronic, mechanical, photocopying, recording or otherwise), without the prior permission of both the copyright owner and the above publisher of this book.

The scanning, uploading, and distribution of this book via the Internet or via any other means without the permission of the publisher is illegal and punishable by law. Please purchase only authorized electronic editions and do not participate in or encourage electronic piracy of copyrightable materials. Your support of the author's rights is appreciated.

FREE OFFER

Find out more about the author by visiting DanBrown.tv

AND to get your FREE Online Marketing Course (worth $197), go to http://goo.gl/rp6vT8

FREE OFFER

Table of Contents

1. Introduction To Continuous Continuity Cash
2. Creating Your Membership Site
3. Choosing The Most Effective Membership Model
4. Finding The Right Membership Software
5. Creating A Finished & Polished Membership Site
6. Launching Your Continuity Website
7. Traffic Strategies

1. Introduction To Continuous Continuity Cash

When it comes to building an online business, there are many different types of ways and vehicles to choose from that it can often become overwhelming and confusing as to where you should begin.

From affiliate marketing, CPA all the way to developing your own high-value information products, there are many different paths that, for the most part, all lead in different directions.

Out of the many different business models that I've explored over the years, one of the most profitable, consistent, and profitable long-term ventures involves creating high-value membership websites, otherwise known as "continuity sites".

With continuity sites you're able to not only generate recurring payments for every subscriber that becomes a member, but you're also able to build credibility with a wider amount of people in your industry because members recognize you as an authority as well as a source for quality information.

This valuable expert status will provide you with a powerful springboard that will enable you to eventually launch other products, websites and opportunities to an existing base of targeted customers that you have already developed a working relationship with.

After all, if someone is willing to pay a monthly subscription to access information about a specific topic, it's likely that they will be willing to purchase other relevant products, or services that serve as components to your main membership site.

However, there is often a misconception that prevents new business owners and entrepreneurs from venturing into the continuity marketplace. For some reason, many people are misled into believing that membership based websites are simply too difficult, expensive or time consuming to create and maintain.

After all, you first need to purchase a membership script or software that will power your site and help you effectively manage the different areas of your community, but you also need to provide subscribers with fresh quality content also.

For many, these little hurdles end many hopes and dreams.

But NOT for you!

Where this part of building a successful membership site is what prevents many from going any further...

Thankfully, it doesn't have to be so difficult.

There are many different ways that you can build a successful membership website without having to spend a lot of time or money.

In fact, since membership websites are so flexible in terms of how they can be structured, you can build community sites that aren't entirely focused on content at all, but instead offer training, personal coaching, community access (masterminds) or tools & resources on segments of your market.

This way, you can design your membership website around your own preferences, schedule and what you are most comfortable working with.

You could also create a membership website based around monthly updates so that you're able to free up your time throughout the month, while still providing consistent value to your subscribers on a regular basis.

Regardless what market you are interested in catering to, you can build a profitable membership site around that niche, and this report will show you some of the best methods for creating successful continuity sites quickly and easily.

So let's sharpen the axe shall we?

2. Creating Your Membership Site

Every website begins with a theme. A theme is a specific topic or focus that your membership website will focus on.

While you could create a membership website that carries a broad theme, they are often harder to maintain, and when it comes to creating targeted marketing campaigns, the more focused your membership site is, the easier it will be to tap into your customer base and recruit subscribers to your site.

Before you can choose a theme or topic for your membership site, you will need to conduct a thorough market research so that you can be able to evaluate the viability of creating a membership site within a specific market that interests you.

While membership sites vary from small micro markets to larger mainstream markets, you want to make sure that your topic will attract enough subscribers to make it a profitable venture, while also paying attention to the level of existing competition in your market.

You want to make sure that you can find a unique 'point of entre', so that you can generate exposure for your membership site regardless of the competition.

Here are a few questions to ask yourself when evaluating potential topics for your membership site, including:

1) Are there existing continuity sites within the market?

You want to build your continuity site around a viable market, and by determining whether there are successful membership sites already catering to your market, you will maximize your chances of building a membership website that will be widely accepted and of interest to the majority of your customer base.

For example, if during your research you determine that there is a pretty low number of continuity site that target a certain topic, it's a strong indication that the market is too small to accommodate too many membership sites.

While smaller niche markets can be very profitable, in order to scale (grow) your membership website you want to focus on broader markets.

2) Do you have the ability to provide quality information and resources to this market that aren't already being offered all in one spot?

Just because you've confirmed that a market is a viable one doesn't mean that you will be able to create a successful continuity site for that market, unless you have the ability to create content that your subscribers will be interested in paying for.

Consider the costs of outsourcing content for different markets, as the more popular a topic the greater number of quality freelancers there are to choose from.

If your topic is too focused or specific, you might find it difficult to locate qualified freelancers who have enough experience to produce high quality content for your members.

Developing a membership website that offers specialized content is a great way to develop a USP (Unique Selling Proposition) so that you stand out in your market, attract subscribers, and win repeat business from your customers so they choose you over the competition every time.

3) How can you offer something new to an existing customer base? (developing & expanding your USP)

If you have established that a specific market is actively purchasing and subscribing to similar continuity sites, you need to determine your unique point of entry into the market.

How can you create a community of your own that offers something different than what other membership sites are offering? How can you offer distinct value in your own membership program?

You need to set yourself apart from other memberships in the marketplace by first defining your USP. Actually coming out in your marketing and telling people why your membership is DIFFERENT. Sounds simple, but often overlooked this alone will exponentially increase your results.

Demonstrate how you're different, how your members benefit by being part of your community, and why they should choose you over the competition.

Your USP could be as simple as the delivery methods that you offer, or the format in which your content is made available.

The more types of content you can expose your customers too, the more thorough your site will feel to them, and the happier they'll be which means they will be more inclined to remain members.

Your USP could be as simple as the delivery methods

that you offer, or the format in which your content is made available.

For example, if you find a competing membership site offering PDF only products to members, consider offering both PDF and videos, or audio based versions of the information products that you create. Since people prefer to learn in different ways, by offering all different formats for your trainings you benefit by catering to a wider audience while simultaneously separating yourself from the competition.

4) Is your theme or market considered "evergreen"?

Evergreen topics include subject matter that will still be in demand years from now.

Generally, health wealth and relationships are the safest markets and the most "evergreen".

That's just a guideline. These topics aren't based on fads or temporary trending topics, but rather on stable, long-term markets that have proven themselves as profitable over a long period of time.

Markets that are considered evergreen are: weight loss, parenting, employment, finance, credit, health, hobbies, sports, etc.

It's important that your membership site is designed around a viable topic so that you can build a **long-term membership community.**

After all, you want to focus on a scalable community base that can consistently grow and maximize your overall income, and if you base your membership website around a short-term topic, you will struggle to retain customers after the initial buzz wears off.

Another important thing to keep in mind is the overall size of your target market.

You want to make sure that your membership site will attract enough subscribers to justify the time and work involved in consistently updating the community with fresh content.

Here are a few other things to consider:

1) Will you be able to come up with fresh ideas for future content to ensure that your website stays current and fresh.

2) Is your market scalable with the potential for ongoing growth? Can you create a future value of your customers? Can you offer them upgrade options to further maximize your income, or are options for product creation extremely limited?

3) Is your target audience capable of solving their problems too quickly (making it difficult to retain subscribers), or is your potential topic able to expand so that you can cater to a larger-scale, continuously growing community?

These are just a few things to keep in mind when choosing your membership topic.

Once you have a general idea of where you want to go with the membership theme, drill down further by identifying what you're personally interested in or experienced with that could add on value to your community:

-Are you experienced with a specific tool?
-Are you trained in specific programs or software?
-Are you experienced in a particular hobby or sport?

-Are you knowledgeable regarding a specialized topic in an existing market?

The best membership sites involve and encourage frequent activity from the administrator so the more active you are within your community the easier it will be to bond and develop a relationship with your subscriber base which will encourage member loyalty.

This means that you want your membership topic to be something that you're genuinely interested in or have experience with. You'll also find it much easier to develop content for your site if you have interest in the topic.

Also keep in mind that themed membership sites are always much easier to manage and monetize than generic communities. You want a strict focus on your membership community, so that you can expand on the topics, yet retain an overarching theme.

If you struggle to nail down a topic for your membership site, consider exploring digital marketplaces where you can quickly evaluate potential topics and see what is currently selling.

One of the best sources for evaluating potential membership site topics is found at http://clickbank.com

While Clickbank is mainly for digital products, they also have continuity and membership based sites in dozens of different categories and hundreds of sub-niches. You can locate membership sites by using the advanced search and ticking the 'recurring billing' option and then hitting the search button.

It's beneficial to search through existing membership sites and communities in order to determine how their membership site is structured, what they're offering, the price point, whether they have an affiliate program with affiliate tools (banners, swipe emails, contests, etc.), as well as the specific content they offer and overall value of the site itself.

Then, ask yourself this question:

"How can I improve on their model?"

Can you expand on the topic's coverage and provide additional resources, tools or information.

Keep a pen and paper handy to write down any ideas you come up with as you evaluate existing membership sites in your market.

This will help you thoroughly analyze the existing continuity programs in your niche so that you can create an improved membership site that offers unique value to your own members base.

Additional Niche Research Resources:
-Amazon.com to look at the number of products focusing on your subject matter.
-Spyfu.com for niche research and detailed statistics on keywords as existing Adwords advertisers.
-Google.com/alerts is useful for locating trending or hot topics that could serve as potential ideas for your membership site.

This research takes time yet it's a critical step in effectively evaluating the theme and topic of your membership site so that you can build the very best membership website possible within your market.

When creating your membership site there are many different models that you can choose from, including coaching or training, email newsletters, monthly updates, or you could even choose to set up a "time limited" membership site where subscribers pay to access training materials or weekly courses for a limited time.

Now, in the next chapter we'll go deep into the different

options available to you so that you can choose the most effective format for your site, and begin building it!

3. Choosing The Most Effective Membership Model

When building your own membership site you have a couple different options in terms of exactly how it's structured and designed to operate.

For example, depending on your goals you may want to create a membership site that is short term, where it's designed to offer content on a sequential basis, until the cycle ends, and then the subscription is terminated, and re-starts as new subscribers sign up.

This is most common with email based courses, for example a make money challenge that lasts 30 days or a weight loss challenge that lasts 90. Subscribers sign up for a fixed rate and receive weekly ecourses in their inbox for a period of time. One the ecourse is over, the subscription cycle ends and the subscriber is no longer charged for access to the training.

On the other hand, if you are interested in developing long term membership programs, which is what I recommend, you want to focus on the traditional model where members pay a monthly subscription fee to access content or resources of some kind, where the membership program doesn't end unless the subscriber chooses to terminate their subscription.

To help you evaluate the different membership models, let's take a closer look at the most popular models for some of the more successful membership sites today:

Traditional Membership Model
In this model subscribers pay monthly for regular content updates and new releases.

By far, this is the most common method of building a membership site and is what I recommend.

In most cases, traditional membership sites either offer a $1 or $4.95 trial to join with the cost increasing once the trial offer period expires. This generates immediate interest and encourages visitors to explore the websites offer (this is also a great way to stand out from the competition if they're not offering some sort of trial).

This structure is very successful because you're providing a clear inventive to subscribers and encouraging members to remain subscribed so that they can continue to receive access at a lower rate than future members should you choose to raise the price.

Traditional membership sites are usually updated on the 1st of the month but one savvy tactic is to update halfway through the month so that subscribers don't join at the end of the month only to gain access to two months worth of content.

You should also consider setting up an archive section of your site, so that new members are able to purchase previous releases or updates, rather than gain access to everything.

One thing to keep in mind is that when you launch your membership site and begin to generate subscribers, it's often difficult to switch formats or change delivery times so make sure to do your best to carefully plan out your website early on, so that there is no need for abrupt changes.

Believe it or not, your subscribers will come to rely on the schedule that you choose for your site, and in order to keep consistency and demonstrate your desire to provide a stable, ever-growing community, you need to do your best to thoroughly plan out your entire membership program before it even launches.

Coaching Base Membership Model
Coaching based training programs typically offer members the opportunity to receive training or personal assistance for a flat

fee, although there are membership based coaching sites that charge on a monthly basis for continued access to new training modules or lessons.

With a coaching based membership site, lessons are made available only to members of the site, with schedules accessible for all members to see meeting times, personal coaching sessions, and live calls.

Coaching can include:
-Personal Training (one on one sessions)
-Group Session Training (webinars, conference calls, forums, etc.)
-Ecourse Training (delivery of lessons by email)

You need to be aware that you will need to address a specific skill level, or experience level so that you can ensure members understand and apply the information your provide in your course. Be careful enough to survey what potential members are interested in so that you can gauge the overall demand and interest and create a targeted coaching program.

Coaching based membership sites are extremely easy to set up because unlike traditional membership sites where you'll need to develop and publish content prior to your website's launch, with service based membership sites you can post updates less frequently, creating content and resources only as the site grows.

Email Based Membership Model
With an email based membership you're able to set up complete membership sites quickly, with very little start-up costs or work involved. After all, since the majority of the content will be delivered by email you don't really need membership software to manage your program.

You just need the resources to create the sales material after you determine a delivery schedule that goes out on the same day each week.

When it comes to frequency, the most common formats include eCourses sent weekly, bi weekly, or (bi) monthly.

Ecourses are profitable because you can minimize the workload involved in launching your membership program. You only need an email marketing service otherwise known as an autoresponder, and to the best of my knowledge [Aweber](#) is the most reliable and cheapest and it's what I would recommend. Other than that all you need is the first month of content, and a way of accepting payment for each subscription.

The easiest way to set up an email based membership site is to create a simple subscription page that features a subscription button (you can create these directly in your PayPal account). When a visitor to your site decides to enroll in your ecourse training, they can either choose to subscribe to a monthly payment plan, where they receive one new module every month, or a one-time fixed rate for the entire product.

4. Finding The Right Membership Software

In order to set up your membership site you will want to first evaluate the different membership software available on the market and choose the one that will offer you the most flexibility.

Membership software is an important part of a successful subscription site because they can handle everything from payment processing, to ensuring that your content is delivered on time based on your programs schedule.

Software also makes it easier for you to effectively manage and update your website, as most professional membership software comes bundled with everything from user management tools, to powerful page builders, and administration options that help keep your site up and running efficiently.

You want the membership software that powers your site to be flexible, scalable and able to handle a large amount of data. That way, you don't need to worry about any problems later on when your membership site grows.

Before you choose a membership software for your website, you need to identify what kind of offers you plan to implement into your community so that you can purchase the right tool to get the job done.

For example, certain membership software only protect user areas, but fail to provide you with the ability to offer one time offers, up-sell offers or integrate a backend system into your website.

Just the same, certain membership software only allow for one level memberships, while other provide you with the option to set up ulti-level programs, so that your subscribers can upgrade their accounts to access additional areas.

Depending on how large or detailed your membership site will be, you may need different functionality from your membership software, so spend some time evaluating the different options on the marketplace. **I've spent hours researching what works best for me and after extensive testing of customer retention I've come to a cost-effective solution that I highly suggest:**

[Effective Conversion Pages & Membership Websites](#)

If you aren't sure how to develop or design a membership website, consider using Wordpress as the CMS (Content Management System) to organize and manage your entire website.

With the [OP 2.0](#) theme (or [plugin](#)) you can create all the different marketing pages you will ever need including full membership websites and launch funnels. You can also take advantage of their blogging theme as well if you don't have your own theme already.

Using OP your customers can purchase modules inside of their membership that will automatically run a script within Wordpress which upgrades them to a higher billing level and charges their card on file seamlessly pushing them up money pyramid.

Regardless of the software that you choose to power your membership site, there are a handful of features you will most likely want to make sure are included, even if you don't intend on using them straight away, chances are, you'll want to implement them later on in order to maximize revenue.

Features To Look For:

1: Drip Feed Content

Drip fed content enables you to create and schedule posts, pages, modules, and/or updates so that they appear on scheduled times and dates. This is exceptionally helpful in planning out your updates and in saving time by publishing content in advance and setting it to appear only on the day your site updates.

2: Unlimited Membership Levels

Your membership site software should offer you the option of creating various levels (Bronze, Silver, Gold, Platinum, etc) so that you can offer extended upgrades and upsell offers to your subscriber base as your website grows.

For example, you could offer "Group A" with access to certain areas of your site for $9.95 a month or fixed rate, while "Group B" can access all of the areas that "Group A" can and also the extended resources, tools and content areas for an additional $29.95 a month.

Having the ability to assign levels is also important in the event you want to feature a temporary offer or a special update that is not part of your regular membership program.

Then you can advertise the offer to your subscribers and allow them to purchase access for a limited time.

3: Sequential Content Delivery

Depending on your setup, you may want to graduate your members from one level to the next. For example, a member joins your site today and receives access to one module. Then, your sequential delivery system would deliver the next module only after the subscriber has been active for a week (or another period of time).

This is a great way to build a training program that automatically delivers content based on where, in the training your subscriber is. This is how to get your clients results as fast as possible by pushing and prodding them through each portion of the training and having them take action on it at chunks at a time to avoid overwhelming them.

4: Autoresponder Integration

It's important that your membership software captures visitors and your members information so that you can send follow up emails, promotions and frequent updates of specifically targeted to where they are in your "marketing funnel".

List building is essential to building a relationship with your subscribers and maximizing your member retention rates. The more frequently you communicate with your subscriber base by offering new releases, features, updates, the more likely your members will remain active.

It's also a good idea to notify your member's base of an upcoming update, in the event you plan to archive the previous months release. That way members can download or view the content before it's pulled off the site.

You can also use this email system to survey your members to determine what they are interested in receiving with future updates. This information is incredibly valuable in order for you to create a membership program tailored towards your target audience, and to ensure that your subscribers remain active members.

The biggest benefit of surveying your members is that you have proven sellers for upcoming products you create and offer in-house to your list.

5: Integrate With Affiliate Program

It's also necessary that your membership software offers the ability to integrate with your affiliate program so that you're able to encourage others to promote your website to earn commissions.

Most membership software integrate with popular affiliate programs like Clickbank and InfusionSoft where you can choose to make all members affiliates or you can allow members to choose to enroll.

And trust me when I say this, if you provide great content, your members can become some of your best affiliates.

6: The Option to Scale Your Website
You need to make sure that the membership software you choose will allow for your community to grow, and is equipped and able to handle large amounts of data and frequent activity. Not every membership software is powerful enough to handle a lot of database activity, so be careful to choose a membership solution that has been thoroughly tested and proven to accommodate large membership communities.

One quick and easy method of building full-scale membership sites is by integrating membership software like [OptimizePress 2.0](#) into a Wordpress based website.

This way, your site will be fully optimized for search engines, while you're able to benefit from a full featured content management solution. If you aren't experienced in developing websites or fiddling around with HTML and CSS code, setting up a Wordpress based membership site with Optimizepress removes all of the tedious work and time consuming learning curve it takes to create a high converting marketing site.

In order to bridge your membership content and seamlessly integrate it into a membership access portal OptimizePress is the "Rolls Royce" of membership software for the SmartCar price.

Once you've chosen your membership software and theme, you will need to register a domain name and set up a hosting account that will house your subscription center.

[HostGator](#) is the most affordable and best option for hosting your website and it's what I use for all of my "money sites".

Just make sure that you choose memorable and preferably a benefit-based domain name that truly represents your niche market. You want people to remember your domain and have little trouble spelling it. Try to use keywords whenever possible not only to attract targeted visitors but to help rank you website at the top of the search engines without added effort

5. Creating A Finished & Polished Membership Site

Your membership site will generate a steady and consistent income from within its own community based on the model you choose, yet in order to maximize your income you should begin to develop a back-end system so that you can increase the value of every person who comes in contact with your business.

Consider how you can integrate different options that would appeal to your members, or integrate various levels into your membership community so that active subscribers are given extended options or benefits by upgrading their accounts to access different areas of your site.

Consider creating up-sell offers, one time offers or other back-end offers that compliment your membership program, and add extra value.

You should also use urgency-based strategies, such as time sensitive offers, or limited spots or memberships left within your community. This will motivate your visitors to take action and subscribe before the offer ends.

You can also offer coupon codes with only a specific amount of them available before expiring.

When it comes to continuity sites there are a few things you'll want to integrate into your model to maximize your profits, and retain subscribers.

One of the best ways to entice visitors into becoming paid members is by offering what is known as 'teaser content', which showcases snippets of content on the main site in order to convert visitors into become paid subscribers.

In [OP 2.0](#) this feature is called the "breadcrumb trail" and could boost revenue by 4x which means you win repeat business, seamlessly pushing subscribers up money pyramid by offering them extra content.

You will also want to pre-determine your content schedule and let it be known to members. This way, you can stay on track with updates and have clear defined deadlines to meet. If you ever have to change your update schedule be sure to notify your members so they're aware of the changes.

Other ways to monetize your membership sites:

-**Feature An Affiliate Program**: Attract affiliate partners who promote your products in return for a pre-determined commission percentage of the sale.

-**Sell Ads Within Your Membership Site**: Membership sites are the perfect place to sell out ad space because the ad buyers know that they are advertising to a targeted group of buyers and not just prospects or freebie-seekers.

-**Post Affiliate Ads Within Your Membership Site**: Posting affiliate banners inside of your membership areas is a great way to monetize your real estate because your buyers will most likely be interested in related offers and when they buy you earn a commission.

-**List/Email Promotions**: Your customer list is by far your biggest asset in your business. Your customers already have a track record of doing business with you and in the "results business" they hopefully already trust you and see you as not only an authority but someone to who they want to engage in repeat business with because you bring value and deliver on what you promise.

-**Keep Customers Engaged By Continuously Interacting With Them**: Interacting with your customers is a great way to come up with product ideas, ideas for high-ticket coaching programs you offer to a few people, and for fostering a deeper relationship with your community.

6. Launching Your Continuity Website

The best way to jump-start your membership site is by building a mailing list of people who are interested in the topic that your membership site is focused on.

To begin, you should set up a "squeeze page" or "optin page" where visitors enter in their information in return for a certain benefit, usually a free download or video series.

You could also offer incentives such as a discount code sent via email immediately after the subscriber opens your email.

Once a visitor joins your list they are automatically subscribed to your newsletter, your autoresponder should send out the first email in your "follow-up" sequence where they will learn more information about your membership site, as well as receive the incentive offer that you advertise on your squeeze page.

You're in full control of how often your follow up emails go out to subscribers, and you can continue to add content into your autoresponder system as often as you like making your followup more effective.

FollowUp Campaign Example:
4 emails that are scheduled to be delivered accordingly:

1st Email: Instantly send an email out to people thanking them for becoming a subscriber and giving them the offer that you featured on your squeeze page or landing page.

2nd Email: Scheduled to be sent out on the 2nd or third day after your subscriber has confirmed their request, and includes an email offering free content, additional resources, or another free report or blog post.

You can also could have a "soft pitch" at the end of the email or in the post script that reminds subscribers who have failed to register for paid membership that your offer will expire if they fail to take advantage within a specified time frame, completely optional though.

3rd Email: Scheduled to go out on the 6th or 7th day of the sequence reminds your prospect how they will benefit as a paid member of your site. Use testimonials if you have any.

You could offer additional free resources including an overview of the benefits and features with your continuity site.

4th Email: Sent out on the 9th day another email encouraging members to join your site before the deal expires, include testimonials if possible, even some of the content inside of the members area as teaser content.

...and so on.

The balance that you should use when mixing up free content with promotional based material is entirely up to you yet the more value you give to your list for free the easier and faster it will be to develop a relationship with subscribers so that they trust your recommendations and look forward to receiving your future emails.

You can see what a campaign looks like at the end of this book you'll have an opportunity to become a subscriber to my newsletter.

It makes sense to look at how large companies break down their content to advertising frequency... Guess what, ESPN sells 9 minutes and 27 seconds of commercials per hour, that's an 84/16%

The Discovery Channel sells 10 minutes and 59 seconds of commercials per hour. That's 82/18.

Some folks err too much on the lean side. I've seen guys with popular blogs and email lists who promise to never pitch you on anything. That's a big mistake. You have every right to earn something for your efforts; it's not like you're running a charity.

Your intention should always be to help your subscribers as much as possible though. I really hope that you aren't that type of person.

It's up to you to keep a pulse on your subscriber base and determine what works best, how frequently to contact them, and whether they respond well to the products you're promoting.

Don't be afraid to experiment and test out new ideas and innovative ways to consistently grow and maintain your subscriber base.

Constantly testing different sources of traffic, and testing which sources produce the most profit is a must.

7. Traffic Strategies

At this point your membership site is successfully set up and all you need is traffic to bring visitors to your website.

Traffic is the most controversial and overwhelming topic to master as a beginner. However, it's actually really simple if you stick with 1 or 2 ways and optimize your campaigns for that source of traffic, then move on to different sources.

I like to use both free residual ways and paid ways to generate traffic. If you have a budget for traffic I would suggest purchasing traffic to test out your offer and different aspects of your sales funnel profitability, but you can benefit from both.

The choice is yours

Now this only graces the surface of what can really be done with a continuity website. If you follow the steps in this report and set up your own continuity site, or if you already own a membership site and make a few tweaks here and there to increase your profits, you will be on the fast-track to creating a steady recurring income online.

Fast Action Steps:

1) Decide on a niche
2) Map out your membership model
3) Use [OP 2.0](#) to Build A High-Growth Membership Website
4) Send All Traffic To Your Lead Capture Pages

There you have it, 4 steps to setting up a reliable and steady income for yourself.

I hope you've enjoyed this membership report. I really tried my best to pack in as much value in here as possible. Yet, to fit everything about creating consistent business and repeat sales into these book pages is an impossible task.

But, if you want to learn more about the ultimate online profit model, coveted secrets like:

-What is The Dot Com Lifestyle?

-The 3 Ultimate Online Profit Models

-How To Create Your Own Information Product (it's not what you think!)

- the single factor that drives you down the path of "execution paralysis" and procrastination…

-Your Own Sales Funnel Worth $10,000

-Your Own Bonus Package Worth $4,997

-Titanium Mastermind Bonus Day Worth $1,997

Then:

[ELIMINATE Your Obstacles And UNLEASH Your Full Potential Here:](http://InternetLifestyleSecrets.com/uopm)

http://InternetLifestyleSecrets.com/uopm

If you want to know **the ONE, must-have skill you need** to create life-altering breakthroughs… the kind that can transform your business from a pit of endless frustration into a launch-pad to freedom and prosperity…

I'd like to send you a copy of my most powerful report that explains everything you need to know about the ultimate online profit model. --- Absolutely Free.

To Prosperity And Beyond!

Dan

www.ingramcontent.com/pod-product-compliance
Lightning Source LLC
Chambersburg PA
CBHW041609180526
45159CB00002BC/791